Eddi
Money Ma   ...ile

Eddie Obeng's
Money Making Machine

Eddie Obeng

eddie_obeng@pentaclethevbs.com

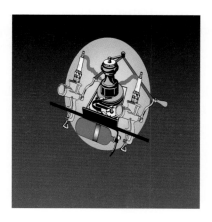

PENTACLE WORKS
THE VIRTUAL MEDIA COMPANY

PentacleTheVBS.com/Money_Making_Machine.htm

Copyright © Eddie Obeng 2002

The right of Eddie Obeng to be identified as the author
of this work has been asserted in accordance with the
Copyright, Designs and Patents Act 1988

First published 2002 by
Pentacle Works The Virtual Media Company
Burke Lodge
20 London End
Beaconsfield
Bucks HP9 2JH

A CIP catalogue record for this book is available from
the British Library

ISBN 095348692-3

Cover artwork by Ian Moore

Typeset by
Sparks Computer Solutions Ltd, Oxford
http://www.sparks.co.uk
Printed and bound by
Alden Press Ltd, Oxford and Northampton

For all the people who have heard
the tale of the Fat, Greedy,
Cigar-Smoking Capitalist

and

my deamon* Susan

*Philip Pullman, *Northern Lights.*

Dr Eddie Obeng at Pentacle The Virtual Business School has created an effective and simple way of focusing you and your business on activities which guarantee success and improve your ability to make money. *Eddie Obeng's Money Making Machine* is in two parts. The first part explains the new approach and how to apply his thinking to your goals. The second part links the processes for making money to traditional measures and explains how to develop new measures and strategies for making money more effectively in our fast-paced, complex, global New World.

Eddie Obeng and his team of virtual tutors will work with you and the key executives, managers and leaders in your organisation to help make the thinking in this book part of your culture. Alternatively, you can find out more about the New World management approach (NMA) and how it applies to your organisation by contacting Pentacle. Dr Obeng also provides regular audio broadcasts/web casts and answers business specific questions through Pentacle's electronic clubs.

If you wish to join other leading thinkers and NuvoMondists who are reinventing their enterprises visit http://PentacleTheVBS.com

Pentacle The Virtual Business School
Burke Lodge, 20 London End,
Beaconsfield, Bucks HP9 2JH
Tel +44 1494 678 555
Fax +44 1494 671 291

E-mail mmm@pentaclethevbs.com

Web PentacleTheVBS.com/
MoneyMakingMachine.htm

Contents

About the Author

EDDIE OBENG pioneered the concept of the NEW WORLD throughout the 1990s. He focuses on helping businesses create and deliver business strategies that allow people to work together to their fullest potential in appropriate virtual organisational structures, using e-enabled information and knowledge to achieve business success in this dynamic New World economy.

Dr Obeng is Founder Director of Pentacle The Virtual Business School (1994), one of the world's most innovative e-learning businesses. He was previously an Executive Director at Ashridge Management College, having begun his career with Shell.

Describing his books, *The Daily Telegraph* said, 'He has a backlist of book titles in a style far removed from the ponderous approach of most management tomes'. As the author of a series of books that describe his philosophy for managing in the New World – *New Rules for the New World, All Change!, The Project Leader's Secret Handbook, Putting Strategy to Work, Making Re-engineering Happen, Soundbytes, Achieving Organisational Magic* and *Cybersense* – he writes on the full range of management topics. He is also a major contributor to the *Financial Times Handbook of Management* and *The Gower Handbook of Training and Development.*

In the *Financial Times* he was described as an 'agent provocateur' and a 'leading revolutionary'. *Human Resources* magazine named him as a 'rising guru' and a 'man to watch for the millennium'. *The Daily Telegraph* described him as the 'Max Headroom' of the business school world and 'unusual to back his own ideas with his own money'. And *The Sunday Times* described his Pentacle The Virtual Business School as 'one of the few which combine continuous learning with remote management'.

Eddie regularly presents his New World philosophy concepts and success stories to large audiences. His presentations have been described as 'As energetic as Tom Peters but not as long ...' by *Human Resources Magazine*.

Eddie is also a regular contributor to journals, magazines and TV.

Other books by Eddie Obeng in the New World Library:

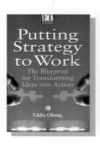

Why?

I've wanted to write this book for a long time. I began my personal quest to rediscover and re-invent a business management approach relevant for the world we live in (rather than the industrial/post-industrial management theories I learnt on my MBA) by writing *All Change!*

All Change! was, I hoped, a business book with a difference – part narrative/part text book – no case studies, no name dropping, just 'NuvoMondism', my brand name for the management philosophy I was trying to create. *All Change!* introduced my alter ego, Franck, who you will meet again here. Franck then joined me for *Putting Strategy to Work, New Rules for the New World, Making Re-engineering Happen*, but failed to appear in

Soundbytes and *Never Reorganise Again!* Each book was on a different area of business enterprise management. And now, to this book, one that I've wanted to write for a long time.

When I first started teaching my New World Management Approach (NMA) I used to contrast the way of thinking and behaving in the Old and New Worlds. I did this by inviting participants to pretend to be and to think like a 'Fat, greedy, cigar-smoking capitalist'. I would then encourage them to think about the best ways to make money and even more money in the Old and New Worlds. I was constantly amazed that, time after time and even to this day, most managers and executives only have a hazy, if any, view of how organisations actually make any money. As a rule someone always suggests that businesses make money by 'adding value'. To me this is just like shouting 'Rumpelstiltskin!' (from a fairy tale you may have come across when you were growing up) – using words to name a phenomenon you don't understand.

The idea of the ArgentMeter™ came from some work I did with Nuclear Electric (now British Energy). We were trying to get the staff to increase their business acumen and were trying to think up ways of making the commercial effects of electricity generation more obvious. I suggested having a great big chart in the entrance lobby which showed what had been generated at each site each day. Instead they produced a large 'clock' showing the daily generation.

So at last I get to write about money. I hope that you learn from this how to make more of it more easily, but be sure to read the story to the end to find out **The Fifth Question**. Make sure you discover *what is even more important than money.*

Enjoy.

Eddie Obeng
Balcons de Pralong
January 2002

A 'True' Story about Discovering the Money Making Machine

Chapter 1

The Meeting

In which the problems of trying to deliver results in the New World are discussed and understood.

It's gone.

'Message for delivery to 2/persons.'

In a single swift movement I've picked up my coat and keys and slipped on my jacket, grabbed the handle of my brown leather case, slipped my PDA into my jacket pocket and pressed 'start-u-s-return' in rapid succession and I'm out of here.

What has prompted my bat-out-of-hell exit is that again as usual I'm late. … And I've got so much to do. It seems to be the norm these days. The meeting

overran – largely because the guy on
the audio link began a 30-minute
monologue which no one could break
into. We were supposed to be solving
the business challenges and discussing
how best to meet the lowered targets.
Instead all we got was a 30-minute
diatribe from an overenthusiastic VP.
And as a result I didn't manage to get
the revised quarterly figures off and
have spent the past half-hour replying
to e-mails and phone messages, chasing
for the numbers. If only I'd got it off in
time I could have saved all the effort
of reassurance. Everyone is worrying
about how the job cuts will affect them.
And there is so much to do … and I can't
remember where I put the PowerPoint
slides of last week's resource meeting
… and with the layoff announcements
I need to resubmit my estimates. The
last four minutes in the office were a
desperate but unsuccessful scramble to
try to find the e-mail they were attached

to … I brake sharply avoiding the driver of a green Range Rover who has swerved unexpectedly. I zoom past him cursing slightly under my breath and noticing in an instant that he's talking on his mobile. I guess I'm not the only one trying to get more done than I have time for. I'll have to get them to send the PowerPoint e-mail again. I reach for my own 'hands-free' phone. Just before I touch the green dial button it rings. I spend 15 minutes on a call which is of no real value to me and simply reminds me that there is so much more I have to do.

Now I'm pulling up on a high street of buildings that look untouched by time. Outside my car it's still somewhere circa 1500. The road between the rows of buildings is wide, too wide, about five lanes wide but the road itself only takes up two lanes outside the buildings. Between the trees parking is perpendicular, and free. I still can't spot the 'It's really easy to find. It's a large cream building with a large black coach door. You can't possibly miss it!' that I'm looking for. I find a parking spot and continue my search in haste on foot.

'So why do you think you have this huge workload?' he asks gently.

I'm sitting in a wooden beamed room at a round table looking out over the high street I was so recently driving along. I've missed my slot of the first coffee break and now my colleagues will be tied up with a computer simulation on their course for the next hour. So I have half an hour to kill before I can do my bit on the course providing the business context and strategic update and answering any pressing questions. I have half an hour to kill which I am passing by chatting away to one of the business educators at the business school. I reply, 'The real problem is that I find that I keep agreeing to do things or be accountable for things.'

'So you say "yes" out of the goodness of your heart?'

'Not really, it's just that sometimes I don't really know what is involved. And if I'm … to be honest, sometimes I forget exactly what I have on my plate and am already supposed to be doing. You see, the problem is that they all seem to need doing,' I say, slightly embarrassed at my obvious lack of organisation. I think, 'I really sound pathetic'. So I add, 'So I end up saying "yes" when I should probably be saying "no" or prioritising.'

'SO WHY DO YOU THINK
YOU HAVE THIS HUGE WORKLOAD?'
HE ASKS GENTLY.

'You end up saying "yes" when you should be saying "no"?' he asks curiously with a slight inflection to the end of his sentence, emphasising the word "no". He pauses briefly. 'Why do you do that?' This time his tone is slightly accusing.

I think for a moment and say, 'I guess because, if I'm being really honest, it's because I don't really have a complete idea of all the things I've promised and am supposed to be committed to.' My voice trails off in embarrassment.

But Franck is now relentless in his interrogation. 'What?' he says with incredulity, 'How come you don't have a full idea of what you are already committed to and having to work on?'

'Well, you see,' I say pausing and trying to sound less pathetic than the contents of my words, 'I don't really have time to plan. There's so much going on – and it keeps changing – I have to keep reacting to meetings, e-mails, audio conferences.' I summarise, 'I guess, to be honest, I'm really too busy to plan, and anyway,' I say to justify my conclusion, 'as soon as I've made a plan it gets interrupted by something else and it becomes obsolete. So I just focus on the most critical issue.'

Franck nods understandingly but unsympathetically. He has a slight smile on his face. He asks gingerly, 'Do you find that you often come close to the mark – almost missing deadlines on some of the jobs you have to do?'

'Yes,' I reply, nodding in agreement. Having to respond to executives chasing for information was, after all, one of the main reasons I was late to make my presentation.

'And,' he continues, 'do you find that other people, sensing that you might come very close to their deadlines or even just miss them, do their best to chase progress, often interrupting you?'

I nod energetically. How does he know this? Franck must have been sitting on my shoulder all day to know all this. I say with feeling, 'It's really annoying, but I have to rush to finish off jobs which come close to the deadlines whilst fending off phone calls and e-mails which need replying to, but simply slow you down rather than letting you just get on with the work. I've tried not replying, but staying silent simply prompts even more interruptions and it means that when you do deliver everyone is really fed up with you.'

'Do you also find,' he asks, pausing as if for effect, 'that you spend a lot of your time trying to find notes of previous meetings, getting your self back up to speed and in general restarting half-done jobs?'

I nod vigorously. 'Yes,' I say, 'and what's so annoying about having so many jobs on the go is that having to manage all the paper on your desk and a full in-tray of e-mails just makes it harder to stay on top.'

Now Franck is smiling as if he has a secret joke. His expression makes me feel slightly threatened. He says, 'With all that paper on your desk and with you constantly asking your colleagues to re-send e-mails you send out clear signals, so now people know that you are not in control.' I think, 'This is amazing – how does this guy know what's going on in my world without being there?' He's still talking. 'Guess what? They constantly phone you on your mobile and e-mail you continuously trying

to get to the head of the queue. This
effectively messes up any planning
you've done and adds to your enormous
and ever-growing workload!' He guffaws
as if this is the punch-line of the joke he
has been building up to throughout our
conversation.

He's right. But how did he know? And
now what do I do to get myself out of
the mess? I think all these thoughts but
instead I say, 'It's not funny you know.'

THE BEST WAY TO UNDERSTAND
A COMPLEX INTERACTIVE PROBLEM IS
ONE BUBBLE AT A TIME.

'But it is,' he replies. 'Look, here's a diagram I drew up before I met you.' He pulls out a laminated A4 sheet of yellow circles and red arrows in a swirl on a green background.

It looks complicated. I recoil automatically. He notices and says, 'It's not as complicated as it looks, it's worse!' and then he smiles a warm, friendly smile. 'No, honestly, it's not so complicated, if you take it in one bubble at a time. **The best way to understand a complex interactive problem is one bubble at a time.**' He talks me around it, pointing to one yellow bubble and then following the red arrow round to the next.

He starts with the bubble which says **'I have a huge workload**.' As he follows the red arrow along from tail to tip with his finger he says, '**which means that**,' and then he reads the next yellow bubble

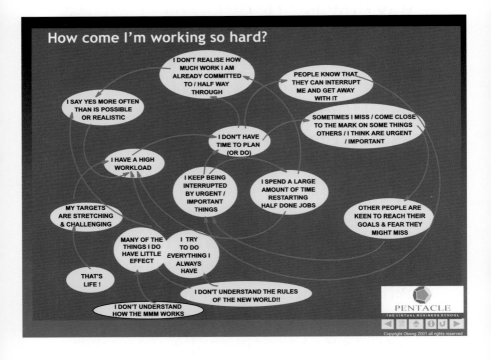

'**I don't really have the time to plan**.'
He pauses briefly and then follows the
next red arrow, '**and as a result**,' now the
yellow bubble, '**I don't realise how much
work I'm already committed to/half
way through**.' He carries on in this way
covering the whole diagram.

'Yes, it's good to focus as you told
me you do, but you must not become
fixated. **Focus but focus frequently**.'

I'm stunned. It's there. It's my life, there
on his diagram. I ask, 'How did you …?'

He interrupts, 'That's not important.
What is important is that **you aren't
the only one who's stuck in this** triple-
nested **set of vicious cycles**. And what
is even more important is finding a way
to get you out of them.' He points to a
pair of bubbles he hadn't previously read
out, one saying '**I don't understand the
New Rules for the New World**' and the

other saying '**I don't understand how the MMM works**.'

I'm slow. My brain is in a jumble. I stare at the diagram. 'What? How? What? Does he? …'. Words start to crystallise, form from the cacophony. 'What New Rules … and what's an MMM?' I ask, raising my head to look directly at Franck, but get no reply. The door bursts open and sixteen of my colleagues pour noisily into the room, thirsty for coffee and to hear from me about the latest strategic moves.

Chapter 2

Doing Lunch

In which I start to understand the problem with money.

It's over. I've updated my colleagues in a quick over-coffee schpiel. They've gone back upstairs, I think to continue simulating, and now it's time for me to go. Time to get back to my turbulent, snowballing workload. I decide to say 'thanks' and 'good-bye' to Franck who seems to have disappeared further into the building. I knock on the door of the adjacent room along and inquire 'Anyone in here seen Franck? – I just wanted to say "good-bye".'

'He's probably in the attic,' replies a lady sitting on what seems to be a large red jigsaw puzzle piece. 'Here,' she says, 'why don't you talk to him.' She picks up the phone and punches in an extension number and then passes me the handset.

'Franck,' I say in staccato, 'I'm just off. The session went very well. I just wanted to thank you for our discussion earlier.'

'No problem,' he replies. 'I enjoyed it. Good luck with your over-workload!' he giggles.

'You never told me what an MMM was or what those rules were.'

'True,' he says. 'Hold on.' I hear a mumbled voice as he talks to someone in the background. 'How are you fixed for a very early lunch?' he asks quickly.

'I'm fine.' I lie, hiding my panic at all the work I was planning to do back at my office.

'Good. Meet me at the front door and we can walk around and get a bite to eat.'

Now we are walking briskly down the high street. Franck is silent and walking half a step ahead of me carrying a golden coloured book in his left hand. I am reading the names of the shops, offices and establishments as we walk past them. An office – 'New Multimedia Consulting', an antique shop – 'Joan's Period Furniture', another antique shop – this one selling jewellery, a pub – 'The Swashbucklers' Arms'. We round the corner to the left; across the road from us is a large Norman church, set in an old graveyard fronted by the village green. Now we pass 'Dancing Feet', a shop selling ballroom accoutrements,

'The Saddlery', and finally we turn into 'The Old Town Teahouse'.

'Table for two,' he requests and in no time we are seated.

Franck starts to speak rapidly as if he has a lot to cover and not enough time to do it in. 'In the past five years, ermmm, decade, in most capitalist, I mean western capitalist economies there has been practically no real organic growth in the top companies – most of the growth has been through acquisitions and mergers – it's called consolidation. Do you know why this has happened?'

I shake my head, wondering where this is leading.

He continues, 'For several complex reasons[1] I won't bore you with here, the pace of change in the business environment has increased. It's increased to the point where now the pace of change in the businessphere[2] is greater than the speed at which organisations can learn what to do and adapt appropriately. This means that many organisations are in a situation where they are constantly surprised by the challenges they face.'

'What', I ask, 'is a businessphere?'

He laughs, 'It's my word for what an industry and its related supply and customer chain turn into, as the edges blur and overlap with other ways of satisfying the same need in the New World,' he explains. 'I keep forgetting it's not in the Oxford Dictionary.'

THE PACE OF CHANGE IN THE
BUSINESSPHERE IS GREATER THAN THE
SPEED AT WHICH ORGANISATIONS
CAN LEARN WHAT TO DO ABOUT IT.

'Never mind,' I reply. 'I know what you mean about being surprised by challenges though.'

'Good!' he responds with relief as if he's pleased he isn't going to have to argue. 'You see, in the situation where your organisation finds that it is constantly being outpaced by events – that is, the world can change faster than you can learn – you have three choices. You can either reinvent yourself to match this New World or try to control the part of the business environment which affects you.'

I nod, following his argument.

'If you decide to reinvent the organisation you are evolving, I call this **evolving for the New World**.'

'Yes,' I think, 'he's got a point. One of the reasons I have so much to do is all the work we've been trying to do to – in the words of our CEO, "adapt to the opportunities and challenges of the New Economy." We're trying to become e-enabled, knowledge managed, customer relationship managed and strategically agile, so far with little success.' I think all this but I say, 'What about the second choice?'

'Ah yes!' he exclaims, 'the second choice. If you go for the second option then the secret is to get really big and to dominate. Dominate your customers, dominate your employees, the governments of the countries you operate in, dominate your competitors, dominate your local labour market. Dominate all the other local brands with your global brand. **When you dominate, you set the terms for your businessphere** – the only threat you have is of antitrust or monopoly action against you by governments – but if you dominate the government, it makes even this action unlikely or, at worst, a prolonged and drawn-out affair. The challenge is that the only way to be sure to dominate is to get big on a global scale – become a world monopoly.'

'I think we've been trying to do both options,' I say slowly. 'We've bought a couple of companies and we had a major merger two years ago which is still working its way through the system. Then it made us the largest business in our sector in this country – now we're back down to number five!'

He nods sympathetically, 'I have a riddle for you. If, when you were smaller, you couldn't adapt and change fast enough, what do you think happens as you multiply in size?'

The answer tumbles out of my mouth easily. It's obvious. 'You definitely won't be able to adapt and change as fast – you'll go even slower.'

He nods encouragingly, adding 'So **along with domination there must be a slowdown in real innovation and reinvention and a reduction in flexibility and responsiveness**. In fact,' he tilts his head and leans forward conspiratorially, lowering his voice, 'this is the hallmark of success in a strategy of domination. You know you have successfully dominated your businessphere when you no longer have to listen to customers. Instead you make them listen to you, make them listen to automated voices and "Greensleeves" playing on unanswered customer service phone lines. You can force them to throw away incompatible competitor software or equipment – wasting their resources whilst locking them into buying your offer.' He smiles warmly and says with a hint of cynicism, 'This, is success!' and laughs throwing back his head.

I respond with slight revulsion. 'That's disgraceful.' I say.

'I didn't say I approved of the strategy. I just said it was one businesses were using. I'll bet your own organisation has its own James-Bond-villain-like "Global Domination Strategy".'

I agree reluctantly, mumbling under my breath. 'What's the third option?' I ask.

'Oh that! It's one I tend not to recommend to clients I like. It's 'Do Nothing Different. Just keep doing what you've always done in the way you've always done it."'

'But isn't that dangerous?'

'No, not really. It just means that your organisation will slowly die, become defunct, diseased and deceased.'

'But that's terrible,' I say.

'That's why I don't usually recommend it to clients. The bigger the organisation, the longer it takes to die; but someone's got to give up the ghost, someone's got to fail so that we can all laugh at them.' He throws back his head and guffaws loudly and then noticing the look of shock on my face adds, 'I'm only joking. I never recommend it to clients,' and then pausing, adds, 'only people I don't like.' And chuckles again.

He summarises, **'I call it "Eddie's Choice", a sort of variant on Hobson's Choice but a better acronym, E.D.D.** It's **Evolve, Dominate or Die**. Most organisations have opted, on balance, for the "dominate" choice whilst trying

unsuccessfully to evolve at the same
time. Mergers are great because often
you can get bigger without it costing
you any cash. Takeovers using share
swaps and the like are even cooler
– a real sleight of hand because again,
you buy something, another company
using other people's perceptions of how
much stronger and dominant you will
be when you have bought them – again
no cash! Tools like these have been
really useful for all the organisations
following the "dominate" route. At
the turn of the century, $3.3 trillion in
2000 (5 times as much as in 1995) was
"spent" on mergers and acquisitions.
The strange thing is that more than half
(about 72%) reported not to have reached
the promised strategic and financial
targets they had set themselves for their
mergers. Strange huh?'

It does seem strange. I think 'Why spend
all that time and money on something

with such a poor chance of immediate success?' I ask, 'So how do you make money on a merger?'

'Although few CEOs would confess to it, for fear of their share prices collapsing, the goal is not to make money immediately but in the far future. You make money through domination.

'Dominating your customers means you can push prices up and the value of the offer down. You can make money by reducing the number of people working for you, i.e. cut out the weakest 10% till the next merger and then repeat. It's a complicated form of the quiz show *The Weakest Link*, in which with each round you survive in the company, you become aware that it is simply a stay of execution, not a reprieve.'

EVOLVE, DOMINATE OR DIE.

'You will notice that dominant companies can employ fewer people in comparison to non-dominant businesses. And because dominance can often generate extra revenues the revenue per employee of a dominant global company can be 10 to 30% higher than the rest of their businessphere. If they wish, they can afford to pay well and attract the best.'

I reply, 'Sounds as if it's worth staying in the company if it promises such over the average rewards.'

'True,' he says solemnly. 'The real problem is that **in each businessphere there is usually only *one* dominant global organisation**, or at best a couple, unless you form an illegal cartel, in which case there will be about half a dozen. So if you're not the dominant organisation, you will eventually be forced to work harder at the first option,

'Evolve to match the New World'. The bigger you are the harder it will be to evolve. And if you can't keep making money as you try to evolve, you will die and be absorbed by another organisation trying to be dominant.'

This is rushing at me. I understood how his argument started but now he's effectively suggesting that in most industries only one or two 800lb gorillas will survive. I challenge him. 'Could you give me some more examples?'

'The dotcom phenomenon was a big lesson in microcosm. Many went for global branding – global dominance. If you didn't try you just weren't bold enough! Few achieved global dominance. Those that succeeded are still major dominant players today. For the rest, there was the feeding frenzy of mergers and acquisitions, attempts to change business models – evolve for the New World – but by this time, many were relatively too big to move fast with evolution and so they expired. Or even now, they are in the doldrums, with downwardly revised profit forecasts and collapsed share prices.'

'I get your point. But does that mean that unless you are in a dominant organisation you're doomed?'

'For the rest of us – the huge majority – those of us who are not working for the dominant organisations we really need to learn quickly how the New World works – what rules it operates to and how to learn and use those rules. And whilst we are learning about the New World, we need to make sure that our businesses can function. We need to make sure that every action helps and makes our businesses more, rather than less, resourceful.'

I nod in agreement. Everything he is saying seems like common sense.

'Making our businesses more resourceful is our real challenge. Most people, especially the senior ones, think that the goal is to increase their power base.'

I nod, smiling.

'What's amusing is that sometimes in the New World they scramble, fight and kick to get more power. And then just as they get it, the organisation's performance collapses below them or they are made redundant. This is almost inevitable since most of the people in our organisations are completely clueless about how the business actually makes money.'

I perk up at this final assertion. 'What?'

'Most managers and executives are more ignorant than month-old babies on how a business actually makes money.'

'I'd challenge that.' I say.

'OK,' he responds placidly, 'you tell me. How, precisely and succinctly, does a business make money?'

My mind races. I don't want to look stupid. I recall something, an expression I've heard. I say, 'Businesses make money by adding value (AV).'

Franck leans forward as if to ask a question, but just at that point there is a tremendous crash. All the heads in the tea shop spin round towards the source of the noise. One of the waitresses has dropped a large plate of cakes.

'So much for adding value,' Franck mumbles.

'Pardon?'

'So!' he says triumphantly, 'that plate of cakes ...'

'Yes,' I respond.

'They were probably baked fresh today. Can you imagine the work – waking up at dawn, getting the flour, adding the sugar, stirring the mix, all the time adding value?'

I nod, wondering where this is leading.

'Putting the mix in a tin and the tin into the oven. Does this add value?'

'Of course.' I respond confidently.

'Baking it, tipping the cakes out, putting them on the plate, all adding value?' He adds an upward inflection to his voice at the end of the sentence.

'Sure.' I reply, reassuringly.

'And now,' he makes a movement with his hands indicating a small explosion and says 'all the added value has been blown up'.

I nod warily.

'Gone. Just like that. All that value. They would have done far better to have kept the plate of cakes in the kitchen and not bothered to serve them to customers and risk them falling on the floor.'

'But that would be stupid,' I protest.

'Why?' he argues. 'At least they would have preserved the added value.'

'But can you imagine it?' I exclaim. 'A cake shop that baked cakes but never sold them? They'd be bust in a month buying all the ingredients and not getting any revenue.'

'So what you are now saying, is that each action they took simply added to their costs. What they were relying on was us, strangers, customers if you like. They were relying on us to turn up and give them some money for some of the cakes, and then they would discover whether or not they had added value.'

Franck continues, 'All the actions you previously said were adding value (AV) – the mixing, the baking and so on – weren't! If they were adding value it wouldn't be necessary to sell the cakes to the customers.'

I'm stunned. There's something wrong with his argument but I can't spot it.

He starts to draw on his napkin. 'You see, in the old world of certainty, of

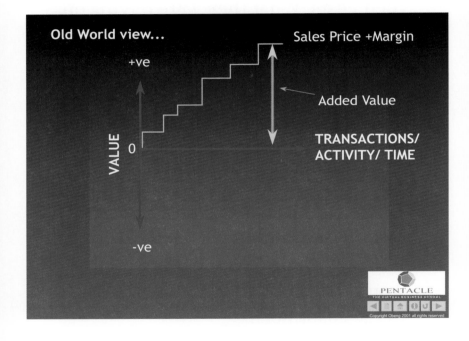

YOU DIG YOURSELF AN ENORMOUS HOLE HOPING THAT SOMEONE ELSE WILL PROVIDE A LADDER FOR YOU TO CLIMB OUT AND THEN YOU KNOW YOU'VE MADE SOME MONEY.

clear industry boundaries, of forecasts valid for more than a week, we could make the assumption that what we made we could sell. The idea was stolen from the traders who invented the idea of accounting – if you are trading goods there is no such thing as a bad trade. So in the Old World convention, every action you carry out adds value, increases your assets, where as in reality it costs you money.

It's only in the New World of change that you realise that your assumptions no longer hold. For example, in the computer hardware industry, because of all the innovation and new developments, you can expect any piece of hardware to go down in price by about 1% per week. Panic-stricken marketing programmes and on-line provision can knock 50% off the price of a product in a day!

'*You* dig yourself an enormous hole hoping that *someone else* will provide a ladder for you to climb out and then you know you've made some money.'

I ponder what he's just said for what feels like an eternity. 'Can he be right? Has the world really changed that much without me noticing?' I try to defend myself. I say, 'Well of course you can only add value by obviously selling at more than you bought it at.' But by now Franck is smiling – I think he feels he's won the argument and I'm feeling peeved.

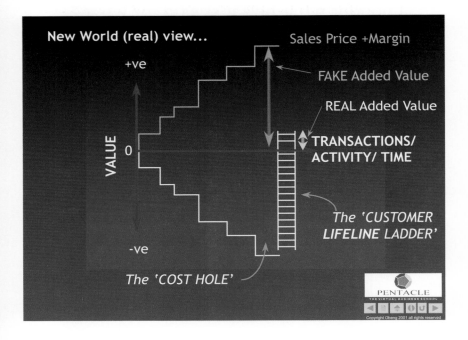

NOTES

1   *New Rules for the New World*, Eddie Obeng,
    Capstone 1997.

2   A businessphere is my word for what, in the
    New World, is the replacement of the concept
    of industry. As it becomes easier and easier
    to find more and more ways of satisfying any
    particular need, the boundaries of industry
    blurr, supermarkets e.g. Tesco compete
    with banks e.g. Barclays, and it becomes
    increasingly easy to find competitors who are
    effective but non-traditional, the concept of an
    industry becomes obsolete.

Chapter 3

The Shop

In which the four of the five focusing questions that are the secret keys to making the Money Making Machine work are discovered.

We finish lunch in a more restful mood. After our discussion about money making, Franck's conversation moved to the weather, flying – I discovered he was a passionate helicopter pilot – and on to the general state of the economy. And there were no further plates of cakes dropped on the floor.

Now we are standing outside the tea shop. We begin our journey back towards Franck's offices and my car. A few paces on and Franck suddenly turns to me and says, 'Hang on, let me introduce you to someone,' he pauses checking, '… if you have the time ...' and with that, instead of continuing back towards the office, he quickly turns right and straight into the shop we are passing. I turn to look into the doorway he's disappeared into. Then I look into the shop window to my left. It's empty, except for a few faded cardboard boxes from a company called TVBS Manufacturing, boxes stamped with a strange logo of a man sitting, knitting on a large golden egg, watched by a large white goose! The white hardboard backdrop prevents me from seeing into the shop. It's obvious that the window hasn't been dressed or cleaned for quite some time. I still don't have a clue what type of shop it is. I glance upwards at the sign above the door, it says, 'Ye Olde MMM Shoppe.' Puzzled, I follow Franck into the cool darkness of the shop eager to find out what an MMM is.

As I enter, Franck is talking animatedly to the shopkeeper, an old man almost bent double, with thick glasses and silver-grey hair. A large pink earpiece nestles in his left ear. As I walk in he turns towards me and asks in a soft but quivering voice, 'How can I help you?' He doesn't seem to realise that I'm with Franck.

'I'm with Franck' I reply pointing at him.

'You're from the Bank?'

'No, I'm with Franck!' I say jabbing my index finger energetically in the air in Franck's direction.

'Aaah. Not from the Bank then?'

Franck steps towards me waving his right arm in a wide sweep and says excitedly, 'This is a great shop. What do you think?'

I glance around the shop. It smells slightly mouldy. Its powder-blue walls are shabby and grimy. In the corner at the back is a pile of precariously stacked brown cardboard boxes. It has an old-fashioned feel – even the till is an old mechanical 'crank the handle' one. All the way around the walls are shelves, shelves struggling under the weight of an assortment of complex-looking machines. The machines look like a cross between an old fashioned typewriter, a grandfather clock and an old clothes mangle. Some are encased in boxes in a range of colours from yellow to blue to green. I haven't a clue what they are. 'What are these things?' I ask.

'What did I bring?' pipes up the old man, shrilly.

Franck leans towards him and enunciates clearly. 'No, he said what are these things?'

'Aaah,' then after a pause he replies, 'they're money making machines.'

'What?' I reply incredulously.

'Money – making – machines,' he enunciates clearly, as if I was the one who was hard of hearing.

'What!' I repeat. 'Is that allowed?'

Franck grins. 'Wrong question,' he says flatly. 'Permission seeking and not even mildly focused.'

Franck is being very rude, but all the same it makes me feel I need to say something else, so I don't look completely dumb. 'I mean, how do they work?' I ask quickly.

'Wrong again,' says Franck unhelpfully.

MONEY MAKING MACHINES.
IS THAT ALLOWED?

'Intellectually stretching but not even vaguely greedy. Come on,' he encourages. 'You're here, standing in a shop that sells Money Making Machines and my good friend here has just asked you how he can help. What is the first question you should ask him?' He looks at me with his eyebrows furrowed as if challenging me to think.

I think for a second but no question forms in my mind. Another second and I ask, 'Why are you selling your machines?'

Franck responds, 'Curious but pointless and not even slightly greedy.'

I'm stumped and starting to get a bit annoyed both with myself and with Franck's attitude. 'Are you telling me the truth? I mean, I didn't know you were allowed to sell money making machines.'

'Seeking reassurance but not even vaguely concentrating on the enterprise goal. Come on,' he says encouragingly, 'you're standing in the middle of a shop which sells money making machines. What's the greedy question?'

'What currency do they make?'

I can tell from his expression that I'm still way off the mark. I try again.

'How much money do they make?'

Franck's face breaks into a broad smile. He says, 'Getting warmer, but look around you,' he gestures expansively at the rows of machines, 'you have a lot of choice.'

'Which one is the best?' I ask timidly with an upward inflection on the last word.

'You were closer before – best could be best in anything – quietest, cleanest, nicest colour. What's the purpose of a money making machine?'

'To make money, I guess.' I say sheepishly.

'Yes! Yes!' he exclaims excitedly.

'Ah!' I say, now convinced I've got it right at last, 'which one makes the most money?'

'But we're in the New World – what does the New World demand?'

Instinctively I reply, 'Speed.'

'Go on. Go on,' he encourages.

'I've got it!' I exclaim. 'Which one makes money fastest!'

'Yeesss!' he responds, hissing out the word and punching a fist into the air as if I've made a major breakthrough.

'But what about reliability? What if they break down or stop working?' I quiz, concerned that my question was far too simplistic.

'I think you'll find that if they break down, the rate of money making goes down too! The fastest machine takes all that into consideration.'

I turn to our shopkeeper and say loudly and clearly. ***'Which one makes money fastest?'***

'Well,' he replies slowly, 'as you can see, I have a range of them. Fastest? Hmmm, well let me see. This one here makes £20 notes, each sheet of the paper costs a pound. It's the only one I have which makes £20 notes. The others in this range make £5 notes. Did I say each sheet of paper costs a pound?'

I nod, grinning. 'I'll go for the £20 machine,' I interrupt, looking at Franck, who seems to be smirking at some sort of private joke. The shopkeeper carries on speaking as he reaches up to the shelf to take down the £20 machine. 'That's right, this £20 machine makes one note an hour, the £5 range all make one note a minute.'

The grin on my face freezes as I realise my mistake. 'I think I'll leave the £20 machine for now. Do you have any machines which make money faster than the £5 range?'

'No, one £5 note a minute is the maximum they come in.'

Franck asks, 'How are you going to choose between the machines in the range?'

'I'm not sure, do they all work?'

'Oh yes,' comes a reassuring reply from the shop keeper.

'How much do they cost, do all the machines in the range cost the same amount?'

'No, different prices across the range. Two bands of prices – the automatics cost about ten percent more than the manuals.'

'Automatics?' I ask, puzzled.

'With the automatics you don't need a full-time, full team of trained technicians on hand all the time.'

I peer at the price tags on the machines. The manual machine costs a cool million, the automatic is a million and a half. Is this right? I'm amazed by the huge price tags and surprised by the difference in price. I can't see an easy way to compare them. I ask the obvious question. 'So how much does a fully trained team of technicians cost?'

'Each year?' Franck interjects. 'I think why the difference. Is this really what they cost to buy? That is NOT the second question to ask in a Money Making Machine shop. You know how fast the money is coming in, what about how fast it's going out?'

I get it. 'Manuals or automatics.' '*How fast must I spend to run the machine?*' I gush in a rush of insight.

'The manuals cost £3.50 per minute, the automatics cost £1.50 …'

I'm lost in my own thoughts trying to do the sums. The automatic will accumulate money much faster than the manual. I figure about five times as fast,[1] but it only costs fifty percent more. The automatic model is probably a better machine for making money.

Franck asks, 'What are you thinking?'

'I think the automatic is the better machine – but it's all theory anyway, I can't afford to buy one outright.'

'So it's not the second question, but, you are right, the "cost to buy the machine is important."'

'Absolutely, I need to know *how much of my own money and resources I need*

to tie up in order to get my hands on the machine.'

Franck nods supportively,

'Say, is this legal?' I ask, worried.

But instead of reassuring me Franck replies, 'Number four!'

'What's number four?'

'You've worked out four of the five questions. Yes, the fourth question in the sequence is to check the compliance issues – it's the ***Am I allowed to do this/ Must I do this*** question.'

'So they are legal?'

'Absolutely. In fact, you probably use or contribute to one every day.'

I can't see that I do, but I say nothing.

The shop keeper interjects. 'So can I interest you in any of my machines?'

I turn to the shopkeeper, 'It's a shame that I can't afford the £5 Automatic machine, but a million and a half is a bit too much for me,' I say in understatement, raising my shoulders in a slight shrug of explanation. **I'd have to borrow to buy it** and I'm sure my bank manager isn't keen on risking, I mean investing, any more money in me.

'No problem,' he says. 'I have just the thing for you.' And with that he disappears behind the stack of brown cardboard boxes in the back corner. He emerges brandishing a gold coloured clock above his head. 'It's my last ArgentMeter™.'

I instinctively ask, 'What's an AahJohnMeetHer?'

IT'S A NEW TIMEPIECE FOR A HARD
WORLD.

'An ArgentMeter™ is a sort of MoneyClock™,' he replies failing to solve my puzzlement. **'It's a New, New World timepiece for a Hard World.'** He pauses as if waiting for me to ask for an explanation. He explains that it's a tool to help you focus in a challenging business world. 'It's usually £25, but for a good friend of my good friend Franck …' He offers it to me in both hands. 'For you, it's a gift.'

I glance at the golden money clock. It looks expensive. I glance at Franck. 'I couldn't, really.'

He insists, 'Go on, take it. You'd make an old man very happy.'

I look to Franck for approval. He nods smiling.

'Thank you,' I say. 'Thank you very much indeed.' We shake hands, and in no time we are back on the pavement outside with me clutching my ArgentMeter™ under my left arm.

NOTES

1   If you're trying to do the sums they look like
     this:

     Rate money in – Rate money out:

     Manuals = (£(5 note – 1 paper) – 3.5 operating)
     = £0.5 made per minute.
     Automatics = (£(5 note – 1 paper) – 1.5 operating)
     = £2.5 made per minute.

Chapter Four

The Short Good-bye

In which I discover where to find Money Making Machines.

'You said that it was legal to own and operate a money making machine.' We are walking slowly back towards my car past the row of shops.

'Of course it is. Your job, the company you work for. What is it, if not a money making machine? And you in your job? You're an operator, part of that technical support team we were talking about earlier.'

I'm pensive. 'I've never thought of a business enterprise as a Money Making Machine before – but hang on, we were almost about to buy a machine in a shop!' I say, 'But you can't say my business is available on sale, down at your local corner shop!'

'Don't forget, people buy and sell businesses all the time. Sometimes it's a share of the business they buy or sell, sometimes it's the whole shebang. Your whole business, your offers, products and services, your processes and your programmes of change and projects, all work in the same way as money making machines.'

I guess he's right. **The whole aim is to make money through the business by working with others in processes and on projects** and he is right, my job is part of the team who make sure that the whole integrated machine works. 'It's a good analogy.' I say, congratulating him.

'Thanks. You're not too shabby yourself. You made it look easy how you worked

out the four key money making
questions.'

'I did?' I respond surprised, unaware I
had achieved this feat.

'Yes, can you remember what you said?'

I can't remember but fortunately Franck
summarises for me.

1   Which one brings in money fastest?

2   How fast must I spend to run it?

3   How much of my money or resources
    must I tie up to have it?

4   Must I do it?/Am I allowed to do it?'

He makes it sound so easy – so simple.
We walk for a few moments in silence. I
feel really pleased with what I've learnt,
but at the back of my mind I know

something is wrong. Something has been forgotten, and then I remember.

Chapter 5

The Fifth Question

In which I learn the value of perspective and discover the most important question of all.

'What's the fifth?'

'Eh?'

'What's the fifth focusing question? You've helped me with four, but you said there were five.'

Franck pauses, 'The Fifth is a bit tricky, it's the most important one and in fact, although you ask it last, **it has the power to cancel or nullify any or all of the first four.**'

'So why do you ask it last?'

'Because if you asked it first, you'd lose your perspective and become incredibly short-termist, and worst of all you would lose all hope. Asking it last does something amazing. It adds real meaning to what you have already decided to do. It will deter you from doing shallow, unethical or morally unacceptable things.'

'Oh.' I reply no wiser. 'What is this question anyway?'

He sighs quietly, as if building strength for what is going to be a tricky explanation. 'Just imagine,' he starts, and then pausing, seems to change his mind and starts again, 'So you remember that, because in the New World the pace of change can outstrip the pace of learning, we decided that we need to think about money not as absolute, but in terms of rates?'

I nod – we've already discussed this.

He continues, 'The rate the money comes in, the rate it goes out and so on.' He pauses waiting for a response and, noticing me nodding, continues, '**Time has become intertwined with money.**'

'Sure,' I say casually. I can't see what the big deal is.

'Imagine,' he challenges 'that you personally became, like, like a cog in the machine, like one of the technicians required to run it, so that all your time all your life was committed to making the machine work – to making money. How would you feel?'

'All my time?' I ask for clarification.

'All your time – you're part of the machine. It can't function without you.'

'No holidays?'

'None at all. Well, not unless you can give me a good reason why you would need a holiday.'

'I'd need a rest.'

'Eight hours sleep every night,' he responds unsympathetically.

'A bit fed up unless I get a chance to spend time with my family.'

'Why do you want to see your family?'

'Because I love them. I enjoy being with them. I like to see what the kids have discovered.'

He says silently, almost secretly, '**Fun and learning**,' and then out loud, 'OK, any other excuses for a break?'

'To see friends.'

'Why do you want to see your friends?'

It seems obvious. I reply quickly, 'To have a laugh and find out what they have been up to.'

He says quietly, under his breath, 'Fun and learning.' Any other reasons you need to get away for a holiday?'

I'm starting to struggle for excuses. 'To see other places and cultures and find out what and how they do things.'

'In other words, to learn.'

'You could say that.'

'So if I summarise your excuse for not spending *all* your time as a cog in the Money Making Machine, it is because you want fun and learning.'

'Yes.' I reply protesting. 'But I want my family and friends to have fun too.'

'And you'd enjoy that?'

I start to answer, and then realise that he's just played a trick on me. 'Touché,' I say, acknowledging his idea.

Franck stops walking, turns to face me to get my full attention, and says seriously, 'In the New World, time and money become more and more interchangeable. In fact, a really serious demographic trend is towards people who have more money than time on their hands. The old capitalist world meant that most of us had more time than money. But in reality **money is infinite**. Think about it, there is always more and more created by banks. And in reality **time is infinite**. At least we think it is. And there is about a hundred million years left before the sun turns into a red giant and engulfs the earth. **But your own time is finite**, and that's why *anything you choose to do to make your life fun or to help you learn must always override the four other focusing questions*. So the fifth, the critical focusing question, the one which overrides all the others is, **Is it fun and will I learn anything?**'

I ponder what I've just heard: 'It all makes complete sense. Even the first four questions now, in retrospect, seem like just good common sense, so why don't we just do it?' I ask, 'So Franck, why don't people just do it?'

A broad smile forms on his face and his eyes take on a misty, dreamy look. He replies, almost in autopilot.

'There are many reasons. The first is lieutenant syndrome – the person who starts the business enterprise never really explains to his lieutenants how it all fits together, but instead uses strict financial controls and more-of-the-same growth measures to manage them. When eventually the lieutenant takes over they simply continue with the controls without an understanding of "Why". After a while, revenue growth becomes confused with market share, and share and global scale, instead of being a means to an end, become the goal itself. The power balance shifts, it becomes more important to have the new or prestigious client than to make money. In many organisations I know, their most prestigious product or client is often one of their worst Money Making Machines. This is often because they've discounted their offer and bent over backwards to get the client's name on their list. They waste money on their prestigious product, and describe the spending as 'strategic investment!' You may not know this, but in the English dictionary 'strategic' is another word for loss-making!'

I guffaw. He's so right.

He powers on almost not pausing for breath. 'Once the purpose of the organisation is lost in this way, the internal game becomes one of self protection, gaining power and clearing space for big egos. First, they simply grow the organisation, doing more-of-the-same and then they notice profits falling off, so they try to increase productivity. They forgot that when you hire new people in the New World you must simultaneously innovate on your processes, to allow the overall organisation to evolve. With 10% more people, try to achieve 30% better results. Hiring new people into old processes is just dumb. New people, new and different processes (for everyone).

I nod slowly. It had never occurred to me to change our working processes as we brought in new people – in our organisation we simply delegate the existing activity or process to the new hires.

Franck continues, 'In addition, because it is easier to influence what you control – things inside the organisation – than to influence things outside the organisation – customers and markets – the powerful people in the organisation often get tempted into "random" cost cutting. They may, in the face of a multi-million pound gap in profit, ban biscuits at meetings. They initiate continuous re-organisation of reporting lines, and travel and telephone bans in search of a cost advantage. Most of the time they forget to check the impact of these internal actions on the external stakeholders, customers and suppliers. Squillions of initiatives aimed at productivity improvement through current processes and infrastructure ensue. I remember once hearing about an organisation which, to save money, moved the staff from two town-centre locations into a tiny out-of-centre office, but forgot that there was another 12 years to run on the city-centre office leases. The city-centre offices have remained empty and fully paid for the five years. It's like the second question, 'How can we reduce the rate at which we spend?' has been asked first and has been the only question asked. But the answer has simply been a panic knee-jerk, which ends up acutely increasing the rate at which they spend! What's worse is that sometimes this over-focus on question two actually damages the ability to bring in more money faster from customers and retain their interest and loyalty beyond the immediate term. It damages the ability to meet the objectives of the first money making question, "What can we do to bring money in faster?"'

I'm thinking, 'This is weird. There seems to be a total misaligned over-focus, whilst the questions needed for focus are so simple and so clear.'

'And then,' he adds, 'as if this were not enough, it all gets legitimised through meaningless slogans, "Speculate to accumulate," "Strategic investment portfolio," "P/E = G," and so on.' He pauses, exhausted from his ranting monologue.

I comment, 'I agree with all you say, but why now, or has it always been like this?'

'Not this bad,' he replies. 'It's just that in the New World, your lack of understanding of the Money Making Machine is quickly exposed.' He pauses and glances at his watch. 'Now you have learnt the five focusing questions, it might be an idea to read about the 12 New Rules for the New World.' And with that, he hands me the golden yellow book he's been carrying. He explains, 'For your continuous learning.'

Chapter 6

The ArgentMeter™

In which I learn how to use an ArgentMeter™.

Now I'm sitting at my desk in our offices, a desk which I have temporarily cleared of all my usual clutter.
In the middle of the desk sits the ArgentMeter™. It looks like a mis-planned clock – instead of the time, it is marked out with concentric rings of numbers. There is bold lettering where the hours would normally be, which spells MONEY-IS-TIME-IS-MONEY-IS-TIME in a never ending cycle. I am reading the strange instruction manual. Strange because the cover states boldly, "New Time Pieces for a Hard World" below a dark surrealistic image.

New Time Pieces for a Hard World

The ArgentMeter (New World Clock)

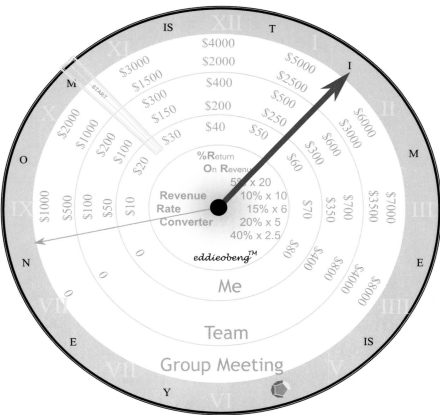

Time is money - literally

'Congratulations on becoming the owner of an ArgentMeter™ {pronounced ar~john~meet~her}.' I smile, recalling asking the old man about the device when I first heard of it. 'It will be invaluable in your quest to become a NuvoMondist.'

The usual sales blurb but this is less intelligible than usual. On the facing page is a picture of the ArgentMeter™ with all the key parts labelled and numbered. It is a picture that I habitually ignore. I ignore it. I go straight to the instructions. 'To use the ArgentMeter™ first enable the batteries and set the machine. To enable the batteries remove the blue pull tag (3). Rotate the knurled knob (7) until the mauve pointer is aligned with the hour hand on your watch. The seconds hand can be set accurately by depressing the knurled knob to stop its motion, (unlike

a clock, the classic ArgentMeter™ has
no minutes hand).

Next, establish Q2* for yourself.
I look at the bottom of the page to
find out what * refers to. It says, 'Q2
of the focusing questions is, "**How
fast must I spend to run the money
making machine?**" To establish this
for yourself, take your annual salary,
multiply it by 3 and divide it by the
number of hours you work a year (1600).
This will tell you approximately how
fast your organisation has to spend to
make sure that you can help run the
money making machine.'

I return to the main text. 'To operate the
ArgentMeter™ slide the circomarker™
…' 'Circomarker?' I say out loud in
incomprehension. Sheepishly, I refer
to the previously ignored diagram of
the named and labelled components.
I discover that the circomarker™ is a

transparent hairline circumferential slide. I return to the instructions. '… slide the circomarker™ to the start time in hours.'

'To convert to revenue use the multipliers in the central circle.'

I don't get it, but fortunately the next section labelled 'Example' promises to help.

'To help you understand how to use our ArgentMeter™ we have provided an example.

'Say you are paid £30,000 per year.

'The rate at which your organisation must spend to allow you to help them run the Money Making Machine is:

'((30,000 × 3)/1600) = £56 per hour

'This means that you would read **Time-is-Money-is-Time** on the scale which is in multiples of £50 for every hour.

'Set the circomarker to the current time. Note the position of the pointer when you finish the task.

'Say the circomarker is at £150 and the pointer is at £350 when you finish, you can calculate that you have spent £200 (= £350 – £150).

'To tell if the task was worth doing you need to find out how much revenue you now have to generate, to get back to where you were in business profitability, before you spent the resource on your task.

'Let us say your business makes a profit of £100 on a sales revenue in the year (last year) of £2000, then its % return on revenue (ROR) is 5% profit on sales.

Look in the central circle for your multiplier. For 5% ROR the multiplier is 20 (= 100/5). This means you need to generate £4000 (multiply your £200 spent on resources by 20), in order for the task to make money sense.'

I finally get it! **The ArgentMeter™ is a tool, a calculator for converting money directly into time or is it time directly into money?** It's to help you focus so that you can spend your time in the best way. What a fantastic idea!

Chapter 7

The Re-visit

In which I discover the keys to making and controlling my own machine.

It's been a strange week. I'm sitting in our conference room alone, but for a lukewarm cup of black coffee and Vanessa. Vanessa is my laptop. I've just finished a meeting, which lasted 37 minutes. Normally our fortnightly budget update meeting takes the nine of us about an hour and a half. 37 minutes and we achieved more and got more focus on what we need to do next to make things work out. Normally all our effort is on defending things which have already gone on and which we can do nothing about.

The past two meetings have been different. I put that down to the enormous poster of Franck's Five

Focusing Questions on one wall and the ArgentMeter™ on the facing wall. In that short time, merely a month, the increase in awareness of the meeting attendees to Money-Is-Time-Is-Money has been phenomenal. For example, instead of saying, 'We've spent fifteen minutes on that topic, can we now have a decision and move on?' people have started saying, 'We've spent £200 on that topic.' Or one person said 'Do you really think we should continue worrying about that topic? I can't see how we will regain the £4000 we've already spent on it.'

For the previous meeting we arranged our agenda using the money making questions. Normally we would start with actions and issues carried forward from the previous meeting. And then we would deal with the urgent or troublesome issues. What I discovered was that this approach meant that the

really brilliant new money making
topics were being squeezed out of the
meeting to the end, when we were tired
and couldn't really give them the time
or commitment for discussion.

It was strange. The first few meetings,
me in the chair testing all our
suggestions and decisions, one at a
time against Franck's Five Focusing
Questions.

It hadn't been easy. I had a revolt from
the Marketing Manager who accused
me of being dogmatic and inflexible and
obsessed with making money. This I
took as a compliment. Gone were the
long tedious diatribes and monologues
and people trying to persuade us to do
things to the detriment of our company.

Franck's questions now shape my 'to
do' list and even the order in which I
return phone calls to customers! But

W A N T E D: More Money

The Five Money Making Machine Focusing Questions...

1. Which action will bring in money fastest?

2. Which action will have the biggest reduction in how fast money goes out to run the business?

3. Which action will release money or free up resource out of the business?

4. Which actions must I do to comply?

5*. Will this action be Fun and will we Learn anything?

* The fifth question overrides all the others

www.pentaclethevbs.com

best of all, I felt absolutely no guilt whatsoever yesterday when I spent the afternoon playing table football, and talking with one of our new hires about the opportunities and challenges of the job that they were taking on. I spent time explaining why we needed new and better processes and outcomes. Not just for him to 'learn the ropes' and repeat the previous generation of learning.

No. I'm wrong. There has been something even better than that. I've convinced my team to change the style of their e-mails. We now start the title line with a number, 1 to 5, representing Franck's Five Focusing Questions, to help the recipient work out what priority they should give to their response. No more of the Old World prioritisation by what is urgent/important. Not only has it cut down the volume of e-mail (cover-your-anatomy mails have just about disappeared!) but it makes it much easier as the recipient to prioritise. It's so simple. I wish I'd met Franck and his Money Making Machine shop-keeper years ago. Think of all the time and angst I could have saved. I take a break from my thoughts and listen to the steady tock-tock of the ArgentMeter™

I wish somehow I could get the rest of the organisation to think in the same way. And then it comes to me. I could get some more posters and I could get a few more ArgentMeters™ and distribute them to other departments. With that I pick up the phone.

Now I'm standing on the corner of the High Street, just around the corner from Franck's office, confused. Cyberspace failed. My phone call to Orange Pages Directory Enquiries drew a blank. Orange Pages couldn't find the phone number of the shop for me, so I decided to come and look for it myself personally in touchspace, and now I've drawn a blank. I've paced up and down the street, twice, and I can't find it!

I could have sworn that the Money Making Machine shop was just a few doors up from the Saddlery but ... I pace back down, but nothing. And then I realise – I don't remember a specialist model shop. I stop in front of it. It could be. Yes it is! With the windows dressed and a new paint job, it is barely recognisable. Of course! It's where the Money Making Machine shop was. It's gone. The MMM shop's gone!

I enter the model shop. Thoughts crowding my head, 'Did they go bust?' 'Was he arrested?' 'Was it all wrong anyway?'

The shop attendant comes up to me and asks, 'How can I help?'

'Do you know what happened to the shop that was here before?'

'Not really. They sold some sort of machinery, there were oil stains all over the floor – we had to take it up and replace it. I think I heard that the owner had moved to the New World, America I guess.'

'Did he leave a forwarding address?' I ask anxiously.

'Not really. I think all we have is a website. Hang on.' With that he disappears under the counter only to emerge a moment later with a folded piece of yellow paper. He offers it to me in both hands. 'For you,' he says, 'Maybe that will give you a start.'

I thank the assistant and step outside. I unfold the sheet, it reads:

HTTP:// WWW.PENTACLETHEVBS.COM/ MONEY_MAKING_MACHINE.HTM

Now I'm sitting at my desk. I've just composed an e-mail ordering twenty posters and a dozen ArgentMeters™. I click on the 'send' button. **'Message for delivery to 1/persons.'** It's gone.

Making Money in the New World

Five facts about Money

1 Money is hard to get hold of. It is **closely interwoven with time** and **someone else has the final decision** over whether or not we make money.

2 Making money is the **effect of actions** and decisions. Money is transient, changes its value constantly and is hard to hold on to.

3 There is always **something** which **stops us making more money**.

4 It's **most useful** as a set of stored promises only **when we ask for the promises to be met**.

5 **It is an illusion** which can distract you from what is really important.

To keep this book short and to provide me with an opportunity for a sequel, *The Money Making Machine Needs More Oil* or *The Return of the Killer Money Making Machine* or similar terrible title, I'm only going to work through the first fact in detail.

MONEY IS HARD TO GET HOLD OF. IT
IS CLOSELY INTERWOVEN WITH TIME
AND SOMEONE ELSE HAS THE FINAL
DECISION OVER WHETHER OR NOT
WE MAKE MONEY.

So where do we get money from?

It seems as if legally there are really only five groups of reasons you can get people to part with their money to you:

1   in exchange for tangible goods or products e.g. a loaf of bread;

2   in exchange for help, advice, enjoyment or information e.g. Disneyland, web site updates;

3   in exchange for a belief, aura, brand, recognition or a sense of belonging e.g. club membership, Mercedes Benz;

4   in exchange for money in the future or to replenish lost money in the future e.g. insurance or

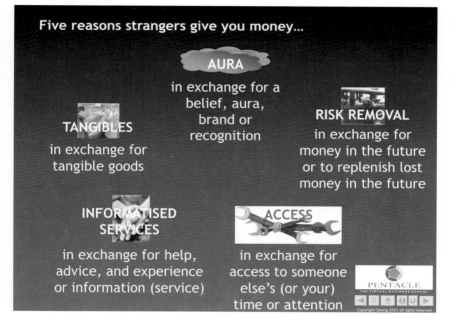

Five reasons strangers give you money...

AURA
in exchange for a belief, aura, brand or recognition

TANGIBLES
in exchange for tangible goods

RISK REMOVAL
in exchange for money in the future or to replenish lost money in the future

INFORMATISED SERVICES
in exchange for help, advice, and experience or information (service)

ACCESS
in exchange for access to someone else's (or your) time or attention

PENTACLE
THE VIRTUAL BUSINESS SCHOOL
Copyright Obeng 2001 all rights reserved

5   in exchange for access to someone else's (or your) time or attention e.g. magazine advertising.

The combination of these five sources of money is what I call **The Offer**.

Understanding where you intend the money that keeps your business enterprise alive is to come from and go to, is the critical part of your business model.

During the dotcom boom, as millions of small, instantly global Internet businesses sprang to life, an important new word was invented. The word was to 'monetise'. It was easy enough to get hold of the initial capital from greedy Old World investors who wanted a piece of the action they didn't understand, but saw it had brought riches to others. It was easy enough to set up websites and easy enough to provide information or services, but how could you actually get any money from them?

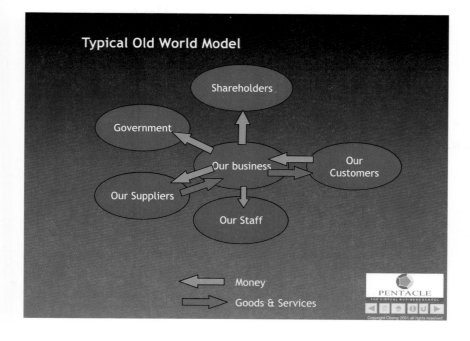

This inability to monetise the offers eventually led to a scramble to reinvent and change their business models as their funding ran out. Unfortunately for most, the process of thinking through the offer and understanding how to monetise it came far too late, and led to the wholesale extinction of the business ventures.

A business model is a representation of the connections between different groupings (called, in the jargon, entities) explaining how the exchanges of goods, services information, access and promises flow.

In the Old World most organisations made use of roughly the same model. As a result, there was little competitive advantage to be gained from your business model and so the differentiating factor was strategy. The similarity influenced the situation almost to the point that many executives are/were unaware of the importance of the business model, in determining the success of the organisation at making money.

And anyway, the syllabuses of most business schools focused almost exclusively on 'strategy'. (In fact, any executive education course with the word 'strategy' in the title was bound to have a significant price premium!) As a result, most senior executives focused on strategy. All this made sense in a more stable business environment where the chances of environmental fit and execution were much higher.

In the complex, fast-changing New World, a wider range of business models can provide opportunities and a stronger competitive position. Partnering with supplier entities or co-opetition with competitive entities in certain market spaces, building complex relationships with suppliers, customers, consumers and clients, and turning them into communities of interaction or influence are all options. Some organisations, notably dotcoms and advertising agencies, have even added exchange and sources of money from the customer's suppliers. For example, you receive a free service on the Internet but your telephone line supplier pays your Internet service company a fee. The source of money is the customer's supplier. ('Cusplier' as I like to call it in humour!)

In the Old World, most transactions and trades were what I call a zero sum. That is to say, imagine I give you the goods, you give me the money. At the end of the transaction I have the money and you have the goods. The sum total was zero because what you received I lost and vice versa.

A BUSINESS MODEL ONLY WORKS
IF IT INCLUDES A REALISTIC AND
SUSTAINABLE ROUTE BY WHICH THE
MONEY COMES IN!

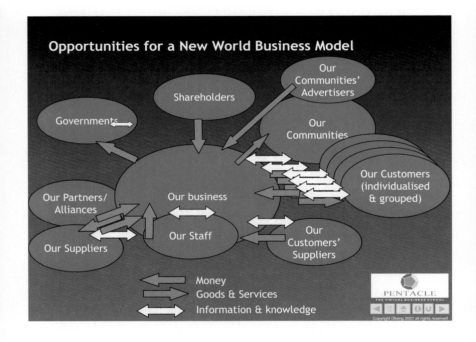

In the New World, the explosive growth of cyberspace has allowed the creation of non-zero sum trades.

Imagine that I had some information or knowledge, say, a software programme and I sold it to you over the web. At the end of the transaction, you would have the information, I would have your money, but I would also have my original copy of the software, and if I worked the transaction well, I would have captured knowledge about you. This is not zero sum! And if I continue, I now have the capacity to sell my software again, or the knowledge you have provided, to someone else. This would then leave me with your money, the second person's money, information about you, information about them, relational information about the two of you. All of this I could then sell on again! Think about this idea every-time you visit amazon.com and you are informed that 'people who bought the book you are browsing also bought ...'

The net result of a non-zero sum transaction is that the more money you make the more you accumulate. You can accumulate information capital, goodwill, market access, etc. To make sure that you hold on to your gains, make the transaction as frictionless as possible and capture all the information you can.

Creating non-zero sum transactions gives you a great opportunity to **bring money into the enterprise faster**.

The other thing to understand about money is that the five groups of reasons people give you money are linked in a really strange way.

I've tried to describe them on the following diagram.

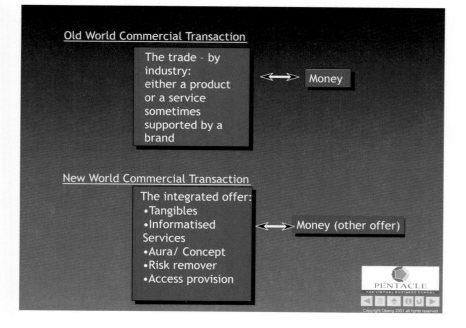

The design of the product and its delivery system directly impact on its usefulness in practice to the person paying for it and its attractiveness. The amount of money exchanged can be multiplied through an effective aura or concept (brand value to the purchaser). The same pattern holds for help, advice or information. The amount appropriate for providing access is dependent on the strength and nature of the relationships to which access is provided. Again an overarching aura will act as a multiplier. Money can also be generated by promising money in the future. The amount people will give you for promises of future money is amplified if you can convince them that the volumes of money created will get bigger through time. This is known in the financial markets as growth!

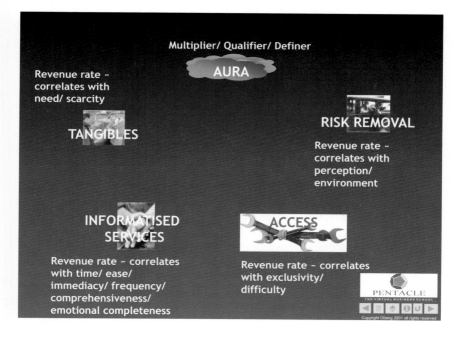

SOMEONE ELSE HAS
THE FINAL DECISION OVER
WHETHER OR NOT WE MAKE MONEY.

In the tea shop Franck and I discussed the concept of adding value. Franck described the process of making cakes and how each step added cost until a customer came along and handed over some money. The chain of activities that the cakes travel along – handed from person to person – is what I call the **Money Making Processes**. The actions are carried out repeatedly **simultaneously** by people across the organisation, but over a period of time the materials, information or customers being processed are transformed. If you're providing tangible goods it's easy to understand how the materials are transformed. Organisations that provide service or information sometimes find it harder to visualise how their customers are processed, transformed from 'people wanting to see the latest movie' to 'satisfied people who can recount the story of the movie in the pub and discuss their favourite parts'. It is still a chain of activities that produces the information or service which has been absorbed or consumed. If you find you can't see the processes in your organsiation, that's just tough! (Or you could read one of my other books – *Making Re-engineering Happen.*)

Apart from processes where people have jobs that repeat every day, the other equivalent route to making money is by stretching out your chain of **activities through time.** Instead of setting up so that people do the same thing every day, simultaneously and simply pass the materials or information on the people they are providing service to, from one to another, get them to do something different on the chain of activities every day. Today is sand digging day – so we all dig sand. Tomorrow is mould-making day so we all make moulds and so on. This **sequential** approach is what I call a Money Making **Project** (or **Programme**).

In reality – compared to the example Franck used and especially in a situation where you are providing service, where people continue to be paid a salary – even if they aren't spending every minute providing the service – the cost hole you dig keeps getting deeper all by itself, as you have to store tangible goods or information, and as you have to pay people just in case their service is needed. In the New World, the other thing you have to bear in mind is that the high speed of change means that, in general, the longer it takes from the time you invent the offer to the time the person gives you money for it, the less they are likely to want to pay for it.

So you've done it! You've managed to get them to part with their money to you once. **How do you get them to do it again?**

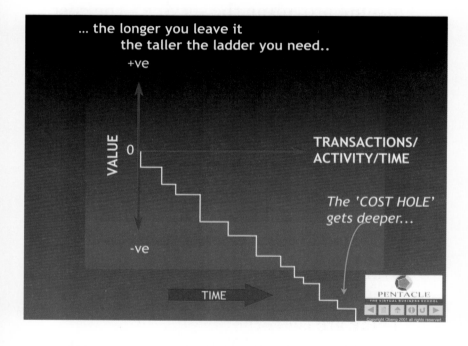

No. Not built in obsolescence – self-destructing software and making your customers miserable are not effective routes to making them come back – not unless the whole industry is rotten, or you have a global monopoly.

To make sure that they come back again and, even more helpfully, that they get other potential customers to come along and give you even more money, you need what I call a **Money Making Loop.**

A money making loop is the use of the New World strategy called CO-EVO (co-evolution).

There are two other New World strategies that are just as valid, and they can all be used together at the same time so you can read more about them in *New Rules for the New World.*

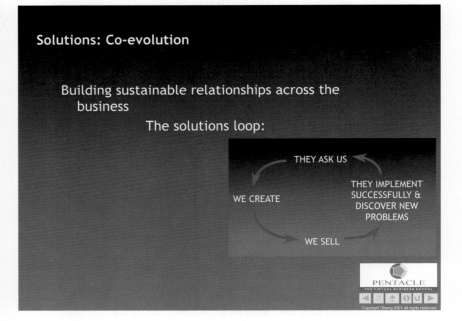

MAKING MONEY IS
THE EFFECT OF ACTIONS AND
DECISIONS.
MONEY IS TRANSIENT,
CHANGES ITS VALUE CONSTANTLY
AND IS HARD TO HOLD ON TO.

ATIF – 'Apple tree in the forest'
– is about providing an offer which is
'irresistibly gorgeous' whilst FROSP
– short for 'frog-spawn' – is about
mindshare. The goal is to capture
mindshare by putting a large number
of offers in front of the customer. Just
like real frog-spawn you acknowledge
that most of the effort will be wasted.
Co-evolution is the one I want to look at
here.

Do you remember the Cold War – not
many people do – it was a fascinating
period of stability in history. America
felt threatened and so it built arms.
So Russia felt threatened, so it built
arms, which then made America feel
threatened, and round the loop we go
again.

So you see, two different entities end up
locked in a constant dance with each
other.

And why? Because of the fact that the loop is closed but also because of a couple of 'anchors'. America believed in capitalism whilst Russia believed in communism.

This led to a curious type of stability. Something called 'dynamic stability', a stability in which there **is tremendous change and yet the key features remain unchanged!**

'So what?' you think. Well, the 'So what?' is, can we get our organisation to do the same thing with our customers? The answer is yes!

There's an example I love of IBM pre-crash explaining how it printed money for a couple of decades.

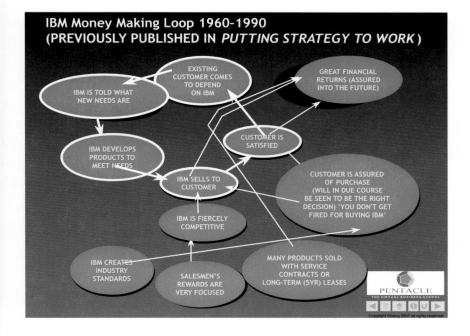

So can you build your own? Of course you can. The basic skeleton of the framework is:

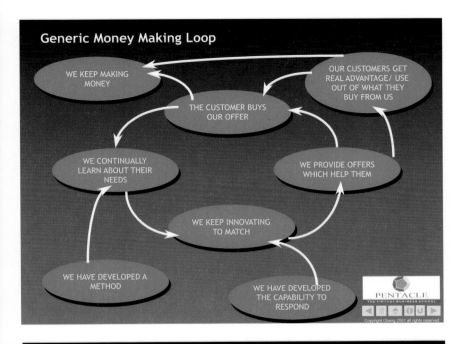

Generic Money Making Loop

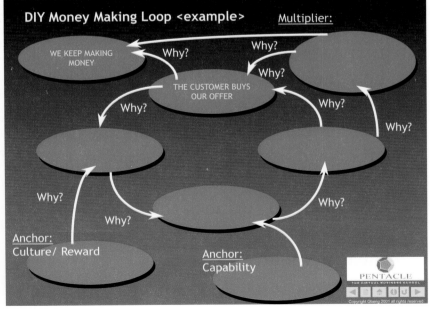

DIY Money Making Loop <example>

Multiplier:

Anchor: Culture/ Reward

Anchor: Capability

Now all you have to do is to fill it in creatively for your organisation, and Voila!

In the Old World we used a number of ideas to work out how much money we had or had made. In the early days this was done infrequently, annually. We would act as though we had stopped the clock after a year at midnight, and would work out for the business enterprise: how much we had accumulated in the period <Profit & Loss>, how much we owned compared to how much we owed <Balance Sheet>, how much cash there was in the bank <Cash flow>. The people who owned the company would find out how much others would pay for their share of the business <Share Valuation/Price>. Obviously the value of the business was expected to be reflected in these measurements.

In the New World you must be bilingual. We use a completely different language for ourselves, and then are forced to translate from New World speak into Old World language in order to trade with Old Worlders.

In the New World all primary measures include time. **At all times have your ArgentMeter™ nearby so that you can convert from time into money and vice versa.**

'Which one, I ask, makes money fastest?'

So how fast does the money come in?

$$\text{Income Rate} = \frac{(\text{Revenue} - \text{Proportional costs})}{\text{Time Beat}^1}$$

'How fast must I spend to run the machine?'

So how fast does the money go out?

$$\text{Outgoing rate} = \frac{\text{Operating costs}}{\text{Time Beat}}$$

(You still need your ArgentMeter™)

'How much of my own money and resources do I need to tie up?'

So how much of our own money and resource does it take?

Owned real resource = Total (owned) resources absorbed in the delivery of money making processes and projects.

Language translation of some concepts from the Old World:

- Budgets are set and monitored **not** by 'Who spent the money?' or 'What it was spent on?' but by '**Why it was spent!**' This forces us to plan and monitor money associated with money making processes and projects (directly linking on effort/

spending with the resulting benefit/
recovery).

- Planning is long AND short term.
  Long term vision or goal; short term
  implementation activities within the
  Forecast Horizon[2].

- Cost allocation is not allowed, only
  internal taxation[3].

- Transfer pricing is outlawed – unless
  a real market exists – alternatively
  the whole end-to-end process is
  measured.

- The concept of investment does
  not exist. Only spending exists.
  Spending can be one off, in tied up
  resources or continuous to keep the
  machine running.

Sounds unusual and different, but it isn't
really. I'll bet your New World intuition

THE MORE COMPLEX THE SITUATION
THE MORE SIMPLE THE SOLUTION
(AND MEASUREMENTS) MUST BE ...

has you running two sets of measures, traditional and the ones you use for co-ordinating and managing reality.

... Finally

... or should it be most importantly ...

Is it FUN and will I (we) LEARN anything?

NOTES

1   The Time Beat is the appropriate time-scale for the business. It may be half an hour for a dentist/five months for an effective constuction company or a week for a timeshare business.

2   The Forecast Horizon is the distance into the future that the organisation can reliably predict. In the New World this is rarely more than three months.

3   Internal tax rates are set in advance of business activity and provide the resource for all the non money making activities (including fun and learning) which the organisation wants to carry out.

Ordering Stuff: Books, Posters, Working ArgentMeters™

There are five questions you're probably asking yourself at this stage:

1   How do I get my hands on an ArgentMeter™ for real?

2   How do I get hold of a poster or postcard of Franck's Five Focusing Questions? (The WANTED MORE MONEY POSTER on page 94.)

3   How do I get hold of more copies of *Eddie Obeng's Money Making Machine?*

4   Is there some course or seminar I can go on to expand and test my

understanding of the ideas and make sure I'm applying them right?

5   When do I get started?

For the first four questions you can contact us at

E-mail: NewWorldstuff@PentacleTheVB S.com
Mail: Pentacle The Virtual Business School, Burke Lodge, London End, Beaconsfield, Bucks, HP9 2JH, UK.
Fax: +44 (0) 1494 671291
Phone: +44 (0) 1494 678555

ArgentMeters cost about £60 each.

Posters cost about £40, postcards are £20 for 10.

Book discounts are available for 50 or more copies.

The Money Making Machine Masterclass covers:
- Some facts about Money in the New World
- How businesses make money
- Profits, Sources of money – The 'whole offer' Operations – Money Making processes and projects
- The special case of information in cyberspace
- Identifying what is stopping your organisation making money faster and putting it right
- How to make sure that your business keeps making money – by design
- Getting your people excited about running a Money Making Machine
- Measuring Monitoring your Money in the New World
- How to turbocharge your Money Making Machine.

5   When do I get started?

NOW!

Index